MW00761453

Little Children's Bible Books

JOSEPH

Retold by Anne de Graaf
Illustrated by José Pérez Montero

B&H
BROADMAN & HOLMAN PUBLISHERS

JOSEPH

Published in 2000 by Broadman & Holman Publishers,
Nashville, Tennessee

Design by Ben Alex
Conceived, designed and produced by Scandinavia Publishing House
Printed in Hong Kong
ISBN 0-8054-2175-0

Dedicated to Pedro Pérez Rollán
and to Charlotte Wijnmaalen

Jacob had twelve sons. Joseph was his favorite. One day Jacob gave him a colorful coat. This made the other brothers jealous.

Jealous is when you want something that's not yours. What color is your favorite piece of clothing?

Have you ever had a dream? What did you dream about?

One night, Joseph dreamed the sun and moon and eleven stars bowed down to him, as if he were a king. His older brothers did not like this. "We'll never bow down to YOU!"

Joseph went to check on his brothers who were watching over the sheep. His brothers took his special coat and threw him in a well.

Can you name the colors in Joseph's special coat?

Joseph's brothers sold him as a slave to some people from the far away land of Egypt.

Have you ever traveled to a far away place? How did you get there?

Joseph worked very hard in Egypt.
The man who owned Joseph put him
in charge of his home and farm.

Do you have chores to do? What are they?

Joseph was tricked by the man's wife and she had him thrown into prison! There he helped two prisoners learn what their dreams meant. He did this with God's help.

What is something you can ask God to help you with?

When Joseph had been in prison for two years, Pharaoh, the king of Egypt, had a dream. Pharaoh heard that Joseph understood dreams and sent for him.

What color is a cow? Can you point to all the cows you can see?

Pharaoh put Joseph in charge of storing food during the seven good years, so there would be food in the seven bad years.

In Pharaoh's dream, seven fat cows crossed the river. Then seven skinny cows crossed and ate the fat cows, but they still stayed skinny!

God helped Joseph understand the dream. Pharaoh praised Joseph's God for helping him understand the dream.

What color is your most favorite food? Guess what mine is?

After thirteen years as a slave, Joseph became a powerful leader in Egypt. People came to him to buy food.

Joseph's brothers came looking for food. They left their youngest brother Benjamin at home with Jacob.

Do you have any brothers or sisters?

Joseph didn't tell his brothers who he was. He ordered them to go home and bring Benjamin to Egypt. Joseph was very happy when he saw his little brother after so many years.

What color are the eyes of the person reading you this story? What color are your eyes?

Joseph gave his brothers food to eat. Then he hid a silver cup in Benjamin's food sack. When the brothers brought it back, Joseph finally told them who he was!

What color is your favorite cup?

Joseph was not mad at his brothers. He forgave them for the mean trick they had played on him so long ago.

Have you ever been
mad at someone?
Did you forgive them?

Jacob and his sons moved to Egypt to be near Joseph. Their family was together again.

What is your favorite color?

A NOTE TO THE big PEOPLE:

The *Little Children's Bible Books* may be your child's first introduction to the Bible, God's Word. This story of *Joseph* makes chapters 37–46 of the book of Genesis spin to life. This is a DO book. Point things out and ask your child to find, seek, say, and discover.

Before you read these stories, pray that your child's little heart would be touched by the love of God. These stories are about planting seeds, having vision, learning right from wrong, and choosing to believe. Pray together after you read this. There's no better way for big people to learn from little people.

A little something fun is said in italics by the narrating animal to make the story come alive. In this DO book, wave, wink, hop, roar, or do any of the other things the stories suggest so this can become a fun time of growing closer.